Read-About® Geography

Mississippi

By Trudi Strain Trueit

Subject Consultant
Clay Williams
Director of Exhibits
Museum of Mississippi History
Jackson, Mississippi

Reading Consultant
Cecilia Minden-Cupp, PhD
Former Director of the Language and Literacy Program
Harvard Graduate School of Education
Cambridge, Massachusetts

Children's Press
An Imprint of Scholastic Inc.
New York   Toronto   London   Auckland   Sydney
Mexico City   New Delhi   Hong Kong
Danbury, Connecticut

Designer: Herman Adler
Photo Researcher: Caroline Anderson
The photo on the cover shows a riverboat on the Mississippi River.

Library of Congress Cataloging-in-Publication Data

Trueit, Trudi Strain.
  Mississippi / Trudi Strain Trueit.
    p. cm. — (Rookie read-about geography)
  Includes index.
  ISBN-13: 978-0-531-12572-4 (lib. bdg.)   978-0-531-16813-4 (pbk.)
  ISBN-0: 0-531-12572-6 (lib. bdg.)   0-531-16813-1 (pbk.)
    1. Mississippi—Juvenile literature. 2. Mississippi—Geography—
Juvenile literature. I. Title. II. Series.
  F341.3.T78 2007
  976.2—dc22
                                            2006017608

SCHOLASTIC, CHILDREN'S PRESS, ROOKIE READ-ABOUT, and associated logos are trademarks and/or registered trademarks of Scholastic Inc.
1 2 3 4 5 6 7 8 9 10 R 17 16 15 14 13 12 11 10 09 08   62

You can smell the sweet
magnolia trees in Mississippi.

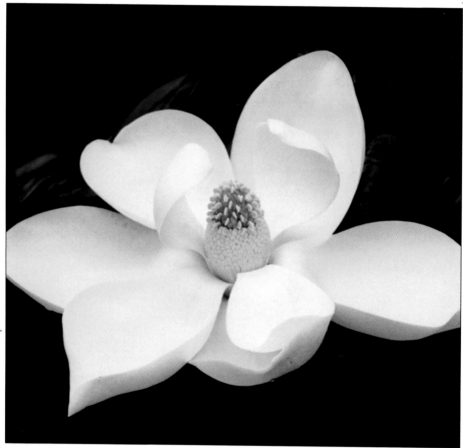

Magnolia blossom

The white magnolia is
Mississippi's state flower.
It is also the state tree.

Mississippi is in the
southern United States. It
is bordered by four states
and the Gulf of Mexico.

Can you find Mississippi
on the map?

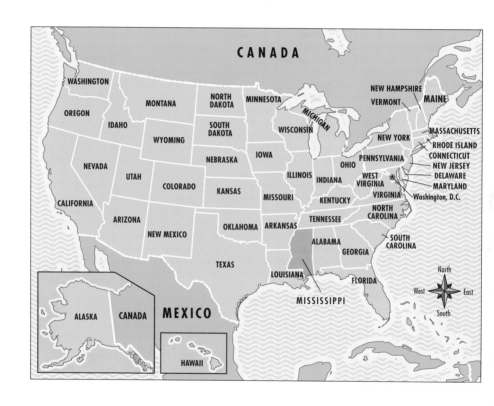

CANADA

WASHINGTON

MONTANA

NORTH DAKOTA

MINNESOTA

NEW HAMPSHIRE

VERMONT

MAINE

OREGON

IDAHO

SOUTH DAKOTA

WISCONSIN

MICHIGAN

NEW YORK

MASSACHUSETTS

WYOMING

RHODE ISLAND

CONNECTICUT

NEVADA

NEBRASKA

IOWA

PENNSYLVANIA

OHIO

NEW JERSEY

UTAH

COLORADO

KANSAS

ILLINOIS

INDIANA

WEST VIRGINIA

DELAWARE

MARYLAND

CALIFORNIA

MISSOURI

KENTUCKY

VIRGINIA

Washington, D.C.

ARIZONA

NEW MEXICO

OKLAHOMA

ARKANSAS

TENNESSEE

NORTH CAROLINA

ALABAMA

SOUTH CAROLINA

GEORGIA

TEXAS

LOUISIANA

MISSISSIPPI

FLORIDA

North

West   East

South

ALASKA

CANADA

MEXICO

HAWAII

5

French explorers sailing down the Mississippi River with their Native American guides

Native Americans were the first people to live in Mississippi.

European explorers arrived in the 1500s and 1600s. Soon, more people came from Europe to settle and farm the land.

Mississippi became a U.S. state in 1817.

Mississippi is a Native American word that means "great river."

The Mississippi River is the largest river in North America. It flows through several states and forms the western border for the state of Mississippi.

The Mississippi River

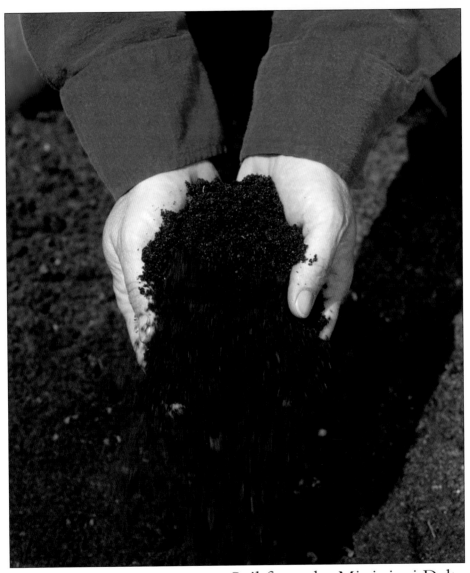

Soil from the Mississippi Delta

The Mississippi River often floods. When this happens, the river dumps rich, dark soil into part of northwestern Mississippi.

This area is called the Mississippi Delta. The delta's soil is excellent for farming.

Much of western Mississippi is flat. It has swampy areas called bayous (BYE-ooz).

The bayous are filled with grasses, trees, and slow-moving streams. Alligators, catfish, frogs, snakes, and turtles live here.

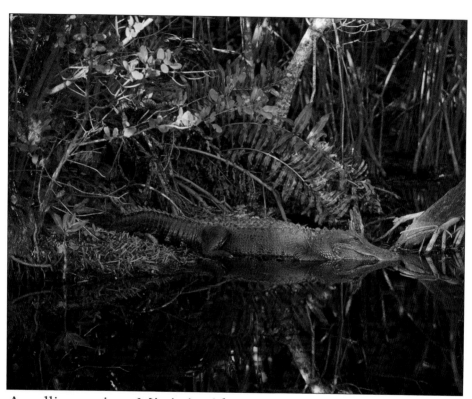

An alligator in a Mississippi bayou

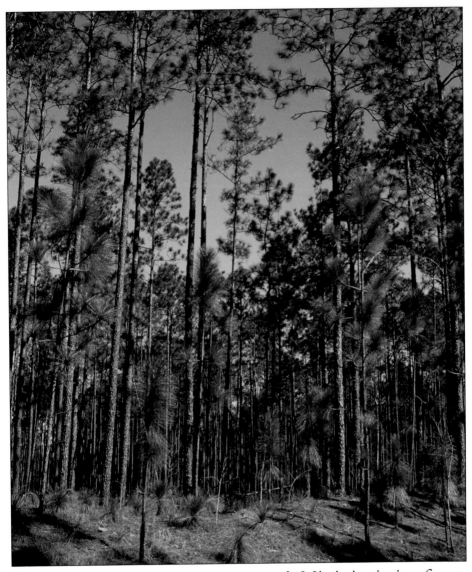

A Mississippi pine forest

Eastern Mississippi has low, rolling hills and pine forests.

Deer, foxes, rabbits, and squirrels make their homes here.

The Gulf of Mexico
borders part of southeastern
Mississippi. Crabs, flounder,
oysters, shrimp, and trout
live in the gulf.

Many people vacation
along the sandy beaches
in this area.

A shrimp

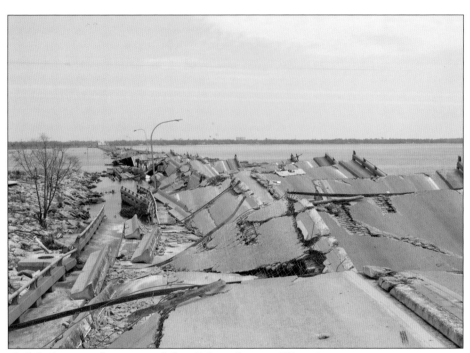

A highway destroyed by Hurricane Katrina

Mississippi's Gulf Coast is sometimes hit by strong ocean storms called hurricanes.

In 2005, Hurricane Katrina nearly destroyed Mississippi's Gulf Coast. People who live here are working together to rebuild their homes and businesses.

Jackson is the capital of Mississippi. It is also the largest city in the state.

Jackson was named after Andrew Jackson, the seventh U.S. president.

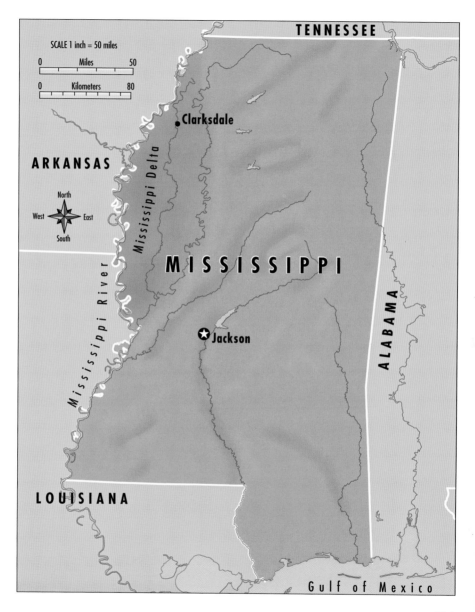

SCALE 1 inch = 50 miles

0   Miles   50

0   Kilometers   80

TENNESSEE

ARKANSAS

Clarksdale

Mississippi Delta

North

West   East

South

Mississippi River

MISSISSIPPI

Jackson

ALABAMA

LOUISIANA

Gulf of Mexico

A Mississippi shipyard

Some Mississippi factories prepare meat and seafood.

Others factories make engines, farm tools, ships, and wood products.

Many Mississippi farmers grow corn, rice, and soybeans.

Cotton is also an important crop.

A Mississippi cotton farmer

Exhibits at the Delta Blues Museum

A type of music called the blues got its start in Mississippi.

You can learn more about this music at the Delta Blues Museum in Clarksdale.

Maybe one day you'll
visit Mississippi.

What will you do first?
You can smell the
magnolia blossoms,
hear the blues, or simply
enjoy a sandy beach!

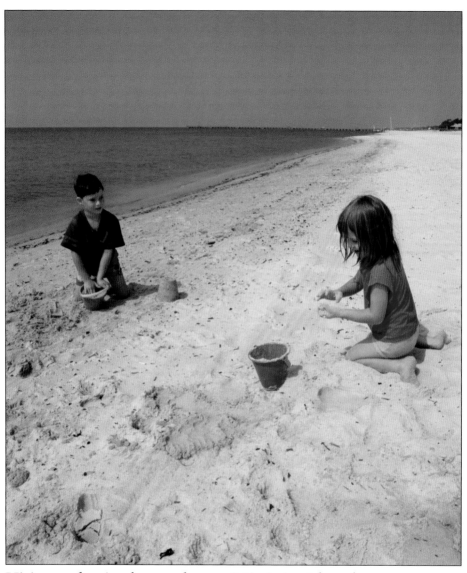

Visitors play in the sand on a Mississippi beach.

Words You Know

alligator

cotton

Gulf of Mexico

magnolia

30

Mississippi River

ships

shrimp

soil

Index

animals, 12, 15, 16
bayous, 12
beaches, 16, 29
blues music, 27, 29
borders, 4, 8, 16
cities, 20, 27
Clarksdale, 27
Delta Blues Museum, 27
explorers, 7
factories, 23
farming, 7, 11, 24
fish, 12, 16
flooding, 11
forests, 15
Gulf Coast, 16, 19
Gulf of Mexico, 16, 19

Hurricane Katrina, 19
Jackson, 20
magnolia trees, 3, 4, 29
Mississippi Delta, 11
Mississippi River, 8, 11
museums, 27
music, 27
Native Americans, 7, 8
pine trees, 15
plants, 12, 15, 24
settlers, 7
state capital, 20
state flower, 4
state name, 8
state tree, 4
statehood, 7

About the Author

Trudi Strain Trueit is a former television news reporter and weather forecaster. She has written more than forty fiction and nonfiction books for children. Ms. Trueit lives near Seattle, Washington.

Photo Credits

Photographs © 2007: Airphoto-Jim Wark: 9, 31 top left; Alamy Images/D.E. "Mac" McGuffee: 3, 30 bottom right; AP/Wide World Photos/Rogelio Solis: 26; Corbis Images: 6 (Bettmann), cover (L. Clark), 18 (Warren Faidley), 29, 30 bottom left (Buddy Mays), 25, 30 top right (Owaki-Kulla), 17, 31 bottom left (Royalty-Free); Index Stock Imagery/Tom Carroll: 22, 31 top right; Minden Pictures/Konrad Wothe: 13, 30 top left; Visuals Unlimited: 10, 31 bottom right (Wally Eberhart), 14 (Glenn Oliver).

Maps by Bob Italiano